Horse Basics

By Kristina Gregersen

Copyright: Kristina Gregersen

All rights reserved.

About the Author

I've been in the equine industry all of my life for one reason or another. I have shown many horses in multiple disciplines, mainly Western and limited English. I've trained, bred, and managed several barns, training facilities, and breeding facilities. I've also worked in tack sales and fitting of tack.

I spend most of my recreation time with my horses. We camp, pack, trail ride and much more.

I'm a certified Equine Appraiser and Equine Consultant, and I've bought and sold many horses. I've volunteered as a 4-H horse leader for 10 years and enjoy working with people and their horses to help them improve their relationship with each other.

Forward

These are some of the simplest but most important things every horse owner should know.

From knowing where all the body parts are, to common blemishes, and different parts of tack, where a horse's blind spots are, common diseases and parasites. All of this and much more will be covered in "Horse Basics."

This is a book specifically for the beginner or horseman looking to add something to their regimen. The topics covered I believe to be very important for any horse owner to know. Since you are reading this book it's obviously important to you as well. And for that you deserve a pat on the back.

Please note that anything regarding veterinary or farrier work, you need to have your own vet instruct you on what is appropriate for your horse and his specific needs. These are just basic guidelines that are very standard; you may need more or less in some cases than what I'm describing in the book. So please use your own discretion.

I hope you enjoy this book and find something helpful or useful to add to your very own personal horsemanship agenda!

Table of Contents

Chapter:

1. As nature intended - 9
2. Parts of the horse - 15
3. Parts of the hoof - 23
4. Common hoof diseases and problems - 29
5. Blemishes - 41
6. Beats of the horse - 47
7. Blind spots - 57
8. Safety positions when working around horses - 61
9. English & Western Saddle parts - 69
10. Headstalls & Halters - 77
11. Basic feeding - 87
12. Common Diseases, Vaccinations & Parasites - 95
13. Closing - 105

Chapter 1

As Nature Intended

The horse has always been my favorite animal. They are complex and simple all at the same time. To be able to fully understand about the equine species would take much more than a lifetime. But, we can take the knowledge we do have and be a better horseman, and it's our duty to be the best horseman we can be, always open to new things and continuously learning.

The horse is one of the most rewarding animals to be involved with; there are so many things you can do with your horse. But, they can also be one of the most difficult, frustrating, and emotional (for you) animals you'll ever meet.

Learning good entry-level horsemanship (along with some great insider tips to care for your horse), can help to develop you as a horseman. As always when starting or improving on anything, beginning with the basics is the best way to success.

As a good horse owner our main task is to make our horse as comfortable, sound and safe as possible. We need to know where all of the parts of the horse are and the function of each one. Understanding this not only will be invaluable if you have a vet visit; knowing when your horse is too heavy on his front end or maybe how to disengage the hind quarters for your safety will just make you a better rider.

Never forget that the horse is considered a prey animal. The fight or flight instinct is very strong in a horse and has preserved it in the wild for a very long time.

As people, we need to be mindful of this instinct when we are handling and working with horses. Even the most broke, gentle, kids' horse still has his instincts deep down and when they get called on, all reason goes out the door and nature takes over to protect and preserve the horse. This is the top priority of every horse.

The main thing every horse longs for above all else is "safety". Nature made them a herd animal. The old saying "There's safety in numbers," is very true for the horse and how they think. That's the main reason a barn sour horse is so common, they feel the safest at the barn or with their buddies in the pasture. So providing a safe environment where the horse feels comfortable is your number one priority as a horse owner. This way you remove any unnecessary stress for your horse. We could all agree, I'm sure, that stress alone can really disrupt your life, health, & relationships. This is especially true for your horse.

Comfort is the second most important thing you can give a horse. After they are safe, the next thing they seek is comfort.

Ideally having your horse with others is best, but if you cannot do that for whatever reason and they are separated, (perhaps for medical reasons or they get picked on or pick on others); you should at least have your facility set up so they can see other horses. This is especially good for their long term health.

Also in the comfort category is room to be a horse. A large area to roam around in is usually ideal. Even if your horse is stalled for extended periods, try and do turnouts regularly (ideally every day). This will usually prevent most stall vices or boredom.

Horses are a grazing animal, in their natural environment they move continuously, eating a little here and there. Horses normally travel around 5-15 miles per day while just eating in the wild. That is a large reason why we end up with horses that have bad habits. Nature intended them to be able to move constantly. When we take them out of that natural environment and put them in a stall or small pen, they must do something with all the excess energy and then vices are created. If you think about it few horses get their 5 or 15 miles a day. Even when exercising on a daily basis you won't cover that much territory unless you work or ride them a long time.

Having a pasture or a large turnout area is invaluable. It still isn't as good as roaming around on a large plain for miles and miles but, at least they get to move around some. This helps to simulate a more natural environment and to keep the horse mentally stimulated as well.

If you have your horse in a lush pasture you'll have to be careful that they don't over eat. A pasture usually has much thicker, lusher grass than a meadow in the woods or prairie would have and they don't have to move around as much to get the right amount of feed.

Even getting a drink isn't much of a challenge. Out in the wild they may have to travel a long ways to get water, compared to wandering over to the corral to get a drink from the water tank.

A grazing muzzle may be a good solution so that they can still get turnout time and exercise while only getting a limited amount of grass.

Having good feed and plenty of fresh water is very important. Naturally getting the correct amount will depend largely on what type of horse you have and its age. I will cover that in more detail later in the book.

The next topic falls directly into the last. Our next most crucial in having a happy horse is "Soundness." If you don't have all four legs correctly working under the horse you simply don't have a horse at all.

Part of being a good horse owner is knowing how to take care of them and when something is wrong. Just like someone knows if their child is hurt, sad, happy, or mad etc.; it's your job to listen, watch, and observe what your horse is telling you.

- Look for changes in behavior or appearance.
  Are they excited to see you come and feed them? If they normally are and they aren't today what is different and why?
- At this point check and see what the problem might be. Start by watching your horse, is he sick? Do a mental checklist of his physical state.
- Is the horse moving normally?
- Always visually inspect your horse whenever you see him.
- How is the horse's body? Are there any obvious signs of hurt or pain?
- Always look on the horse's underside, legs and face for any signs of injury or abnormalities.

Get to know your horse's body, temperament and actions like you do your own. That way any changes are instantly apparent!

A happier, healthier horse makes for a happier, healthier horse owner.

Obviously there are a lot of different opinions on caring for horses and many are worth listening to. Always be open to new ideas and ways of improving yourself. I am always taking clinics, lessons and more to improve my personal horsemanship and ability level. There's always something more to learn.

So, as your knowledge and experience level expands, put

your own regimen together until you get one you're comfortable with.

Chapter 2

Parts of the Horse

Every horse owner should memorize and be able to correctly identify the different parts of their horse. First, if your horse was in pain or injured, could you give an accurate description to your vet?

Second, in order to choose a horse for yourself that will fit and meet the physical requirements needed of him/her you must understand the basics of conformation and understanding confirmation requires knowing the horse's body structure.

Third, there's an old saying that "we know that which we love." Horses make wonderful companions and are responsive to our moods and feelings. If your horse is ever going to be more than just a "tool" to you, you'll want to make the relationship between you and it something special and enduring. That happens best when you know your horse as intimately as you know your own body and soul.

Don't look at the photo and list and get discouraged! Make it fun and figure out a way for you to easily remember the parts of the horse. Sit down and study the diagram of parts then get familiar enough that you can find the parts on your own horse or a horse in a magazine article.

Diagram 1: Parts of the horse.

This is a basic over view. Use this page as a reference point when studying the parts of the horse.

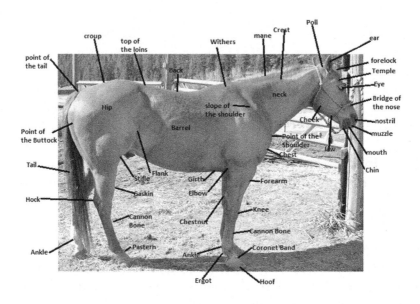

1. Poll
2. Ear
3. Forelock
4. Temple
5. Eye
6. Bridge of the nose
7. Nostril
8. Muzzle
9. Mouth
10. Chin
11. Jaw
12. Cheek
13. Point of the shoulder
14. Chest
15. Slope of the shoulder
16. Forearm
17. Knee
18. Cannon bone
19. Coronet band
20. Hoof
21. Ergo
22. Ankle
23. Chestnut

16

24. Elbow
25. Girth
26. Barrel
27. Flank
28. Stifle
29. Gaskin
30. Pastern
31. Hock
32. Tail
33. Point of the Buttock

34. Point of the Tail
35. Croup
36. Top of the Loins
37. Hip
38. Back
39. Withers
40. Mane
41. Neck
42. Crest

Diagram 2: Sections of the horse.

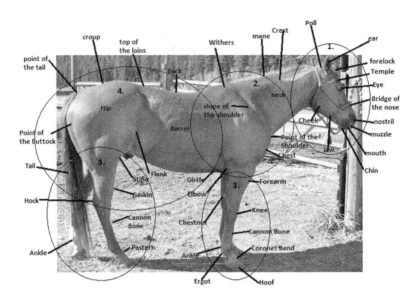

This is a diagram to use when getting familiar with all of the parts. Practice just one section at a time.

- Start with the head only
- Then move to neck
- Next the chest and shoulder
- Now the legs
- Finally the rear of the horse.

Repeat the above process until you can look at just one section of the horse and know where everything is, then move on to the next section.

It really doesn't take all that long to get familiar if you study it for just a couple minutes a day and be consistent in your efforts.

Sometimes having a buddy help you will make the parts stick better in your head. Have your friend point at one of the parts, while you name it like a game or use flash cards.

Diagram 3: Connect the lines to the correct places on the picture.

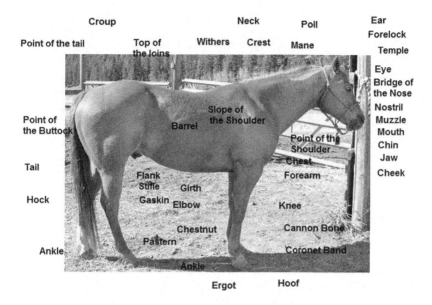

Notes:

19

Diagram 4: Self Test

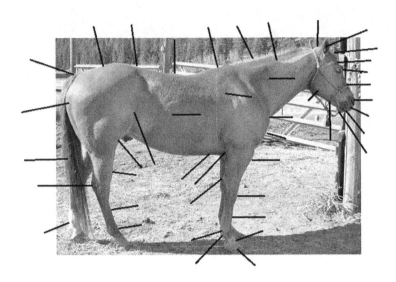

Notes:

You can label your own parts on this page. Try and finish without looking!

Diagram 5

With this picture make your own parts Diagram. Draw your own lines and put down all the parts of the horse.

Chapter 3

Parts of the Hoof

There's a lot of truth to the old saying "if you don't have sound feet you don't have a horse." You need to have strong healthy hooves on your horse to keep them sound and happy.

We will begin by learning the parts of the hoof, and then in the next chapter we will discuss a few common hoof problems.

There are many things that can go wrong with hooves and too many to list in this book alone. If you have hoof problems you need to consult your veterinarian and/or farrier.

What we'll do here is give you a few basic guidelines to help you better understand the hoof structure and some common hoof problems.

Every hoof is shaped just a little different than the other. They are as unique as our finger prints or snowflakes. But, all have the same parts and basic structure.

Typically you will leave hoof care to your farrier such as regular trims and/or shoeing. However, basic maintenance is something every horse owner will have to do with their horse's feet; that includes picking the feet out regularly, and making sure they look good, plus scheduling the farrier to come for a visit. A horse will typically need its feet trimmed every 8-10 weeks depending on the individual.

A good hoof care regimen is crucial in making sure your horse has healthy feet, also having a reputable farrier working on your horse is a must. Poor farrier work can result in a lot of problems for the horse down the line.

Study the following diagram and become familiar with the parts. Then move onto the next pages.

Diagram 1: Parts of the hoof.

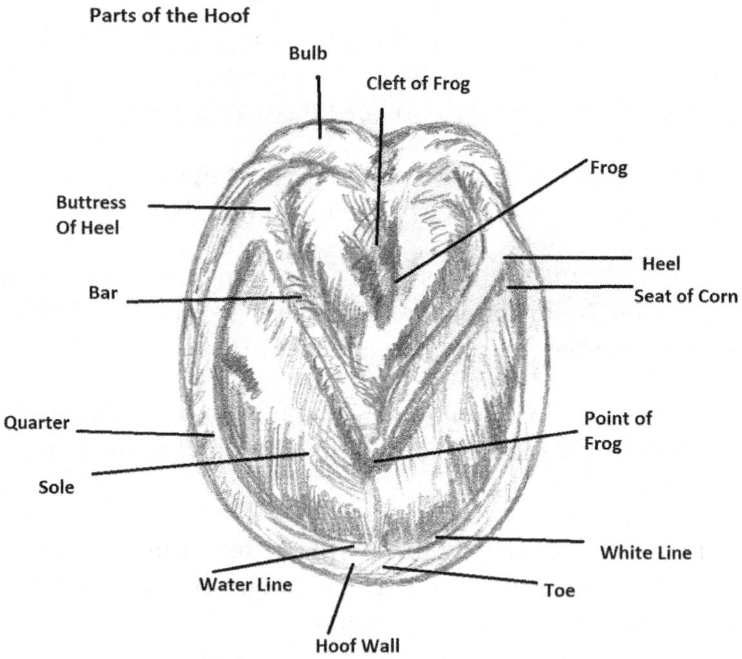

Parts of the hoof:

1. Bulb
2. Cleft of frog
3. Frog
4. Heel
5. Seat of Corn
6. Point of Frog
7. White Line
8. Toe
9. Hoof Wall
10. Water line
11. Sole
12. Quarter
13. Bar
14. Buttress of Heel

    (Refer back to the list above as needed.)

Here is a diagram that is blank. Put the name of the part on the line. Do as many as you can without referring back to Diagram one.

Diagram 2 Parts of the hoof:

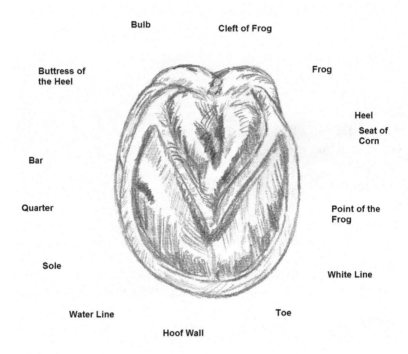

Now with this Diagram put your own parts on the correct line. This will help to familiarize you with the hoof even more!

Diagram 3 Parts of the hoof:

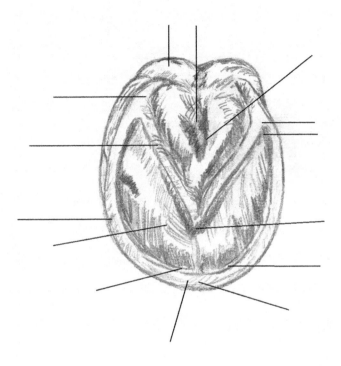

Notes:

Diagram 4 Parts of the hoof:

Now make your own diagram: draw lines and label the parts of the hoof. Have fun with it! Now that you know the parts this will be a cinch!

Chapter 4

Common Hoof Diseases and Problems

In this chapter I'll cover some very common hoof problems and some of the basic causes for those problems. If you experience any kind of hoof problems or health concerns regarding your horse, please seek veterinary and/or help from your farrier as soon as possible. These are basics to give you a good idea of some possible causes and problems you might encounter. Also some ways they may be treated or looked after.

Hoof Abscesses

A hoof abscess is an internal infection of the hoof. The hoof becomes infected and creates "pus" which is nature's defense to rid the body of unwanted foreign matter. The hoof, however, cannot expand and this causes a lot of pressure and pain for the horse.

Your horse can go from perfect one day to "can't hardly stand to bear weight" on the infected hoof the next.

All horses can be subject to hoof abscesses but horses that have heavy/large bodies and small upright hooves tend have more problems than horses with larger hooves to body ratios.

Yet, another ironic part of a hoof abscess is the horse constantly has to stand on the affected hoof. This of course, makes it more painful for the horse. There isn't much you can do about this part.

Some of the signs of a hoof abscess include heat in the limbs or foot, sudden unexplained lameness, swollen leg (from constricting the blood flow to the hoof), and/or mild fever symptoms.

Causes of hoof abscesses can be something sharp penetrating the sole of the hoof and creating an infection; something disturbing the corium or lateral tissue of the hoof. Or the most frequent cause, introduction of bacteria and moisture to the hoof.

Diagnosis is usually simple. If the horse is shod the shoe is removed and the hoof cleaned.

Farriers and veterinarians both commonly use hoof testers to check for signs of abscesses. They are a tool that looks a lot like a large and sturdy set of tongs. They will squeeze the bottom of the hoof in various areas to check for pain levels.

Although with an abscess the entire sole is usually affected (mainly by pressure in the hoof), there will still remain a spot in the hoof that is much more sensitive to the hoof testers. Your veterinarian and farrier will usually check for signs of heat and pain also.

While a hoof abscess can heal on its own, it is not the best course of action. The process will take longer and be much more painful to the horse. Also it could become even more infected and spread further into the complicated tissues of the hoof.

Once the veterinarian or farrier have found the origin of the abscess, and depending on the abscess' location, they can make a small incision into the sole of the hoof and use gravity to help draw the abscess downward and out of the hoof. Usually with this type of abscess healing time is very quick and by keeping it wrapped and clean with drawing agents (usually an Epsom salt poultice), healing could be in as few as 2-5 days.

If the abscess is up towards the bars or elsewhere in the hoof (other than the sole) that cannot be easily accessed, the abscess will usually travel its way up to the coronet band or the bulbs of the heel and make its way out there.

Prevention of abscesses is basically good foot maintenance. Keeping your horse's hooves trimmed properly and maintaining a regular schedule with your farrier is key to prevention. If you suspect an abscess, act quickly. Finding and treating it soon will result in a faster recovery.

Laminitis

(Aka "Founder")

Laminitis is inflammation of the laminae of the foot. The soft tissue structures that attach the coffin bone to the hoof wall.

The inflammation and damage to the laminae causes severe pain and leads to the instability of the coffin bone. In severe cases it can result in complete separation and rotation of the coffin bone.

Laminitis is a very sad state to see any horse in. It is a crippling condition which can be fatal in some cases. Once a horse has acquired laminitis it is very susceptible to get it again.

Signs of laminitis include but, are not limited to:

- Reluctance to move
- A saw horse stance (when attempting to relieve the pain a liminitic horse usually will try and rock all of its weight or most of it to the hindquarters)
- Excessive time spent lying down
- Reacts painfully to hoof testers
- All limbs can be affected but, usually the forelimbs are affected the worst
- Rings on the surface of the hoof wall
- Hoof will look like a bowl with long toes

- Where the coffin bone rotated there will be a bulge in the sole of the foot
- The digital pulses will be strong and rapid

Causes of laminitis:
- Overfeeding on grain. A horse gets out and raids the grain room or someone over feeds it.
- Overfeeding particularly in the spring time. (The carbs in the grasses are increased which can alter the blood flow to the laminae of the foot.)
- Retaining Placenta in mares.
- Blood poisoning.
- Obesity
- Lameness; having lameness in one leg and bearing all the weight on the other can cause laminitis in the good leg.
- Trauma to the hoof area, excessive work on a hard surface.
- Improper hoof care, trimming the hooves wrong.

Diagnosis is usually determined by x-rays taken by your veterinarian. From there they can recommend the best course of action to help your equine friend be as comfortable as possible and discuss the best ways of treatment.

The key to successfully managing laminitis is early detection and working with your vet on an aggressive course for treatment.

Treatment begins with removing the cause of the laminitis. If it's caused from overfeeding the horse needs to be immediately taken out of that scenario. A mare with a retained placenta or a horse with blood poisoning is a medical emergency, contact your vet immediately.

Anti-inflammatory medication will more than likely be prescribed to provide the horse some immediate relief. Your vet will be able to provide the correct dosage to use for your horse.

Affected horses should have lots of soft bedding to stand in, preferably shavings. This will help keep them more comfortable as well. Exercise is not a good thing in the initial treatment of laminitis. Keeping the horse calm is crucial.

Ongoing hoof care is vital, your farrier should work with your vet on the best way to trim or shoe depending on the rotation of the coffin bone.

Ongoing dietary management is crucial in keeping your horse healthy and hopefully preventing another episode of laminitis. Many feeds that say they are "ok" for horses that have laminitis really are not. You need to be careful when choosing a feeding regimen and consult your veterinarian. If you can't consult with your vet immediately then just feeding plain grass hay is your safest course of action until you can consult with your veterinarian.

One other note, even being ill your horse needs to be able to see other horses. This will help them stay calmer and happier during the treatment stage of laminitis. Horses are herd animals and very social. They can become depressed easily when they are alone.

Managing laminitis can be very easy if you stay within your feeding guidelines and are very strict on your hoof care regimen. Your horse will thank you for your extra effort.

Thrush

Thrush is a very common hoof infection occurring mainly in the frog. Thrush causes degeneration of the horn (protective frog callous) and produces a foul smelling, dark-colored discharge. In fact, the most obvious sign of thrush is the odor when you pick your horse's feet.

The areas affected will usually be dark or black in color

and/or moist to the touch, almost spongy. It will easily break, crumble or lift up when you scrape out the hooves with a pick.

Thrush occurs naturally in the horse's living environment so some thrush, yeast and fungi will always exist in a horse's foot (even in horses with perfectly healthy feet). It is also present whenever the hoof is shedding and in the regrowth stages.

Thrush grows best in an environment with little to no oxygen such as wet, muddy and unsanitary conditions. It's a bacteria that can linger and hold on a long time once it gets established. Thrush can migrate deep into the hoof, affecting the sensitive parts of the hoof which will result in lameness. The horse may dislike its feet being picked up and cleaned as well, since the hoof area is much more sensitive.

Thrush becomes a problem when blood supply, movement, hygiene, environment, diet or lack of hoof care is present, creating a perfect growing environment for thrush. Obviously, the best way to prevent thrush is with good hoof care, sanitary conditions and a healthy diet.

Treatment means picking out and cleaning the horse's feet on a daily basis, scrubbing the feet with a disinfectant and warm water, and then coating the underside of the hoof with an iodine solution or a commercial thrush treatment product. Soaking cotton balls with the solution then packing them into the cleft of the hoof is a simple, yet effective, treatment.

Thrush is fairly easy to treat but, it can return easily too. Horses with thrush or horses in danger of contracting it are best kept in a clean and dry pens, pastures or stalls. This will help keep things sanitary for the horse. Cleaning the hooves on a regular basis and sanitary living arrangements are the primary preventive measures against thrush and aid in early detection before the infection gets established.

Cracks in the Hoof

Cracks can occur at any time and are not breed specific. They are also not discipline specific. A crack can vary from only affecting the external wall to involving its full width and the underlying delicate tissues.

Basically cracks create wall instability, and, while most cracks are nothing to worry about, they can become serious.

Horizontal cracks are not nearly as common as vertical cracks. Horizontal cracks are usually from trauma or something else that specifically created them.

While vertical cracks are more common, there are a variety of reasons your horse may get a chip or a crack in their hoof. The horse's diet can be a large factor in having chips or cracks, just like a person that is healthy and has good strong fingernails versus an unhealthy person that does not. Horses are very much the same way. Other contributing factors include: excessive stress, trauma, work load, and losing stability of the bottom of the hoof wall.

Dry weather can also be a large factor; a horse's hooves naturally require moisture to stay strong. Running the water tank over in the dry season can help to keep their feet moist when getting a drink. Hoof oils can also help in dry conditions by restoring the natural oils that are lost.

Long hooves can easily crack or chip, just like long fingernails or toenails. You can prevent this kind of chipping by having a regular schedule with your farrier. This alone will help with all sorts of other problems your horse's hooves may come across as well.

Regular hoof care is a great way to detect problems early on, and with most problems, finding them sooner rather than later is the best plan of all.

Injury is often the culprit behind a horizontal crack. A kick gone wrong either by the horse that now has the crack or by another that placed the kick is usually a good bet. Most of the time these cracks are minor and can heal with little outside assistance. Depending on the severity of the crack you may need a veterinarian or a farrier to treat the injury. This type of crack usually has heat in the hoof (the hoof feels hot).

Sometimes nutritional deficiencies will be the culprit. A good hoof supplement added to a feeding program can help to remedy the problem. If this is your course of action, it will take time to see any results. To regrow a hoof all the way through from the coronet band to the bottom of the hoof, will usually take 8-12 months depending on the individual critter.

If the vertical cracks do not reach the coronet band they can usually be repaired. Burning across a vertical crack can sometimes aid in the stabilization of the area and help prevent the crack from ascending upwards.

If the crack is serious enough to cause destabilization when the horse is moving, you will need to stabilize that hoof. Your farrier can do this by putting a shoe on the cracked hoof and possibly adding a patch to give enough surface area to nail to and bring the hoof plenty of support during the regrowth period.

If the crack runs from the coronet band downward, this is usually an issue of trauma. The horn producing cells at the very top of the hoof have been damaged. If damaged badly this area will most likely not be able to produce hoof any longer and the crack will be with the horse for the remainder of its life.

Navicular

The navicular bone can be found in most mammals, including humans. Navicular itself is a soundness problem for horses. It can be treated and the horse can still often be used normally. The navicular bone is just behind the coffin bone and short pastern bone. Its function is to provide a smooth surface to glide on where the flexor tendon changes angle. The tendon runs down the back of the cannon bone, then bends around the back of the fetlock, between the proximal sesamoid bones, then continues on a sharp turn around the navicular bone and attaches to the bottom of the coffin bone.

Some causes can be compression of the navicular bone. Repeated compression can cause cartilage degeneration, the cartilage becomes flattened over time and thus less springy and shock absorbing.

Tension can also be a large contributing factor in navicular. Some believe that the degeneration process begins from having excessive tension placed on the ligaments.

Also a factor is having the toe strike the ground first; versus the heel and frog taking the main amount of the weight like they are supposed to. Typically this is a result of poor farrier work or poor shoeing and trimming, but can be a conformational factor as well.

Conformational defects such as upright pasterns, small feet, narrow and upright feet, significant downhill/ slopped build, and long toes with short heels may also contribute.

Excessive work such as hard galloping on a regular basis can also be a factor. Jumping is also a common contributor. These activities put greater stress on the tendons and ligaments. They also can cause over-extension of the pastern and coffin joints.

Too much standing is a possible contributor of navicular. This is found mostly in horses that are stalled regularly; with little to no turnout time each day.

Also horses with smaller feet and large bodies such as quarter horses, and thoroughbreds seem to have an increased risk of navicular during their lifetime. This may be a reason why ponies are rarely victims of navicular.

Affected horses seem to display an almost tip-toe effect when walking around. The majority of pain from navicular is in the heels of the horse. The lameness usually affects both feet, but one may be more painful than the other.

The lameness can be made worse, or the horse sored significantly when worked on a hard surface or worked in circles.

Treatment for navicular is difficult. No simple, works-for-all, treatment has been come up with. The degeneration is usually advanced by the time the horse becomes lame; by then the effects are irreversible. Currently the best treatment for navicular is to alleviate the pain and try to slow down the degeneration process as best as possible. Early intervention is key; like many other problems, having a plan to help correct and slow the illness can greatly improve your chances of success.

Horses that have navicular still need some form of regular exercise. They just require a less strenuous form of exercise. Soft footing or swimming is a great exercise. Most horses can still be used frequently with care and respect for how much they can do. You should avoid working the horse on any hard surfaces or for extended periods of time. You also should be careful how much the horse is used for jumping, if at all.

There are several possibilities for treating navicular. One method involves prescription drugs that promote blood flow in the hoof. These are not commonly used because of the need to constantly monitor them and the effects they have on the horse.

Anti-inflammatory drugs are frequently given to help the horse cope with the pain. Especially when upping the horse's work load or changing any exercise regimens.

Palmar digital Neurectomy (aka "Nerving or unnerving") is a controversial treatment for navicular mainly due to the serious side effects. Nerving a horse means they severe the nerves that tell the horse he is in pain. While it can provide relief for the horse it can also cause some serious complications and should be done only as a last resort.

Since the horse can't feel pain in that area of the leg, any injuries may go undetected. Complications can include infection of the wound, continuation of the lameness, (the surgery wasn't successful and they missed some nerves or didn't cut all of the nerves completely; in which case nerves can also regrow), and rupture of the flexor tendon.

Neurectomy is controversial; if you even consider it a possibility you should speak with your veterinarian and get their opinion. The most common misconception about nerving a horse is that it will cure the horse from navicular. It is not a cure; it just covers up the symptoms.

Many times this procedure will make the horse ineligible for competitions and it will greatly reduce the horse's market value.

There is another procedure that isn't very successful but might be considered if other options fail. In this process the ligaments that support the navicular bone are severed; this makes the navicular bone more mobile and reduces stress to other ligaments.

While navicular isn't a good thing, many horses that are diagnosed with it still live useful lives for quite some time. However, in severe cases some horses will end up in early retirement and others will never return to their former level of competition.

The main reason I wanted to include these particular hoof problems in this chapter are to alert you to possible problems and ways of dealing with them.

When you go out with the intention to purchase a horse, knowing the signs of laminitis, the basics of navicular, and how bad a chip or crack really is, are all helpful things in your search criteria, especially when dealing with older, better trained, and safe horses that have been there and done that. You'll see these types of issues more commonly in this group of horses than in younger stock. But don't let this deter you, many horses in this bracket are quite healthy and sound with no problems at all.

    Keep in mind these are just a few possibilities; there are many more out there. These are just a few common problems you may run into when searching for the perfect equine partner.

Chapter 5

Unsoundness and Blemishes in Horses

This chapter is especially important to have at hand when shopping for a horse. We will go over some of the blemishes or unsoundness problems you'll want to be aware of. Study this chapter carefully so you'll know what you are looking at before the time comes to test your knowledge.

The following is a picture I drew to illustrate a blemish prone horse.

Diagram 1: Blemish Prone Horse

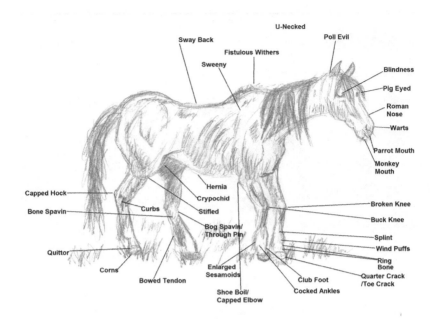

The picture above has almost all the blemishes a horse can have. ☺ The locations of these blemishes are crucial to know if you ever were to run into them.

Although unsoundness and blemishes are usually categorized together they are entirely separate from each other.

Unsoundness for example is something that interferes with the horse's ability to do its work or perform its duty. The unsound horse can no longer work, possibly until the soundness issue is resolved or in certain cases the issue cannot be resolved and is permanent.

Blemishes on the other hand, while not pretty to look at usually don't prohibit the horse from performing its job. These are usually scrapes, or old scars from past injuries.

Unsoundness and Blemishes:

- Poll Evil - inflammation of the poll; a bruise on the top of the poll or persistent irritation. Poll evil can be resolved with treatment. Letting treatment go for too long before correcting the issue can result in permanent scarring.
- Parrot Mouth - is fairly common in a lot of species not just horses. Parrot mouth is where the lower jaw is too short to reach the upper jaw.
- Monkey Mouth - or the undershot jaw is the exact opposite of Parrot Mouth. The under jaw is over shot.
- Blindness - will seriously affect the usefulness of a horse. If you have any suspicions at all about blindness issues or moon blindness problems contact a vet to check and/or confirm.
- Fistulous Withers - Is a swelling of the withers. This condition is much like poll evil. It should be treated immediately otherwise it can linger on with the infection resulting in permanent scarring.
- Sweeny - is a decrease in the size of a muscle. This is most commonly seen along the shoulder muscles; extending from the withers towards the point of the shoulder.
- Sway Back - if a back is swayed bad enough it can affect the horse's ability to be used and can also be painful. This is usually a conformational flaw.
- Shoe Boil/Capped Elbow - blemish at the point of the elbow. Usually caused from a shoe while the horse is lying down.
- Broken Knee - very hard bony enlargement on the front of the knee.
- Buck Knee - where the knee is maintained as always flexed.
- Bowed Tendon - a thickening of the back surface of the leg. This is usually a very serious unsoundness.
- Splints - are simply bony enlargement along the

cannon bone. Usually on the inside of the cannon bone. Commonly young horses are the recipients of splints from rough play or strenuous training.
- Wind Puffs - are a blemish. They are commonly a ring around the ankle or ring around the lower cannon bone. They are common to horses that are used too heavily or trailered a lot.
- Enlarged Sesamoids - bony enlargement of the back of the fetlock joint.
- Ringbone - bony enlargements on the pastern bone. Ringbone is not very common but, a very serious unsoundness. Over time the long and short pastern bones may fuse together, causing severe pain and of course unsoundness.
- Quarter crack/Toe Crack - unsoundness of the hooves.
- Club foot - abnormally upright at the heel with a short upright pastern.
- Hernia - is a gap in the abdominal wall, where organs may protrude under the skin.
- Crypochid - only one testicle is present and the other has failed to drop. This is a conformational fault. Gelding a crypochid is a costly process compared to a standard gelding process.
- Stifled - when the patella of the stifle joint is displaced. If it is displaced outwards severe lameness will occur; if it is displaced inwards and it receives immediate attention you can usually put the joint back in. After a horse has stifled they will be highly prone to it for the rest of their life.
- String Halt - is a disease of the nervous system causing cramps to the back legs. String Halt causes a horse to raise their hocks abnormally high.
- Capped Hock - a large callus on the top of the hock. Usually resulting from trauma to the area.
- Bone Spavin - a bony enlargement at the base and

44

by the inside back border of the hock.
- Bog Spavin/Thorough Pin - soft swellings on the inside front area of the hocks that can result from being joint fluid. Bog spavins are blemishes.
- Curbs - will appear as swelling on the back border of the hock.
- Cocked Ankles - severe strain may result in a shortening of the tendons and create a forward position for the ankles. Advanced cases can even impair movement.
- Corns - usually on the inside of the front feet near the bars of the hoof. Can sometimes ulcerate and cause severe to advanced lameness.
- Roman Nosed - is more a conformational defect than anything else.
- Warts - common in young horses, they are bumps on the nose that usually go away over time.
- Quittor - a decay of the lateral cartilage of the foot. Usually has discharge around the coronet band. It usually creates severe lameness.

Now that we have all the definitions down, here is another chart for you to practice your knowledge on.

Diagram 2: Blemish prone horse.

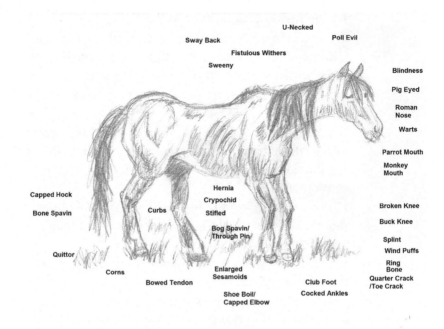

Draw lines to where each unsoundness or blemish comes from.

Chapter 6

Beats of the Horse

The beats of the horse, or gaits, are simply the rhythm and sequence to which a horse places their feet at different speeds.

The gaits can be categorized in two basic groups, the natural gaits and ambling gaits. The natural gaits are simply walk, trot, lope or canter, and gallop. The ambling gaits are in some horses a natural gait but, in others it's a trained gait. We are going to be talking about the horse's most basic and natural gaits, the walk, trot, canter, and gallop.

The gaits are a good thing to learn for basic horsemanship. Knowing how the horse moves and in what order will help you to learn what diagonal you horse is on or which lead to cue your horse to take.

The Walk

The walk is a four beat gait. When the horse begins walking the legs follow this sequence, right hind leg, right front leg, left hind leg, left front leg; in a steady 1,2,3,4 beat. Or reverse the order to left hind leg, left front leg, right hind leg, and right front leg.

The walk is the slowest natural gait and the most comfortable for long periods on both horse and rider.

When the horse is walking there is always one foot raised while the other three are on the ground.

This is a Diagram of the beats at a walk.

The four beats of the horse at the walk:

Note: This can be reversed and will still start with a hind foot, followed by a front foot, followed by a hind, and finally the other front foot.

Fourth Beat:
Left front   **Second Beat:**
Right Front

Third Beat:
Left Hind   **First Beat:**
Right Hind

This diagram can be helpful, the best way to see and hear the beats of the horse is simply to watch and listen to the horse perform them.

The Trot

The trot is a two beat gait that has a lot of variations in speed, but is a very steady movement. The trot can be more of a jog or a working trot pace which is much faster. The trot has a period of suspension in the air.

The horse moves its legs in unison in diagonal pairs, switching from one diagonal to the other. This gait can be difficult for a rider because the body of the horse actually drops a little between beats and bounces back up again when the next set of diagonals strike the ground.

The trot, unlike the canter or gallop (which the horse can only maintain for short periods), can be maintained for hours by a well-toned horse.

Because the trot is a very safe and efficient gait for the horse, a rider should learn how to ride the trot. It is a wonderful gait and a must for any rider that intends to cover distance quickly.

Riders must learn specific skills to be able to sit the trot or they need to learn which diagonal the horse is on so they can successfully post the trot.

The sequence of the trot is right front leg/left hind leg (Beat one), then left front leg/ right hind leg (Beat two).

This is a diagram of the beats at the trot.

The beats of the horse at the trot:
Note: Either side can begin first. This is a diagram to help learn the sequence of the trot.

First Beat:
Left front/Right hind

Second Beat:
Right front/Left hind

The Lope or Canter

The canter is a controlled three beat gait that is usually a little faster than the trot. If you listen when a horse is cantering you can usually hear the three beats. It can sound like someone banged a drum three times quickly.

In the canter the horse is suspended in the air for a moment, the faster the horse is going the longer it remains suspended in the air between strides.

In the canter one of the horse's rear legs-the left hind for example, propels the horse forward. During this movement, the horse is supported completely on that leg while the other three legs are moving forward.

The more extended front leg is matched with a more extended rear leg on the same side of the horse. This is what lead the horse is in; the leading foot in the front and rear on the same side can tell you this information. When you add the weight of a rider it becomes even more important to be aware of which lead your horse is in; especially in an arena or tighter space. As a rider it is important to know your leads and more importantly graduate to being able to feel your leads. This comes with lots of practice and time spent in the saddle.

On a horse that is leading with the front leg and opposite side hind leg, this is called cross-firing or cross-cantering. Cross-firing is when the horse misses his lead either in the front or the back. More commonly the rear leg misses than the front leg. This is a very uncomfortable gait for you and the horse. You will know if your horse is cross-firing. It produces an awkward rolling movement through the horse.

Right lead Canter sequence:

First beat- Left Hind leg, Second beat-right hind leg/left foreleg, Third beat-right foreleg.

This is a diagram of the beats of the horse at the canter.

The beats of the horse at the canter:

The Right Lead Sequence:

Second Beat: **Third Beat:**
Right Hind/Left front   **Right Front**

First Beat:
Left hind leg

Left lead canter sequence:

First beat- Right hind leg, Second beat-Left hind leg/right foreleg, Third beat- left foreleg.

This is a diagram of the beats of the horse at the canter.

Beats of the horse the canter:

Left Lead Sequence:

Third Beat:
Left front leg   **Second Beat:**
Right hind/Left front

      First Beat:
Right hind leg

The Gallop

The gallop is very similar to the canter but, it is a four beat gait, that is faster and more ground covering. The gallop is used by the horse to escape from predators or any type of danger. The gallop is also used in many competitions such as racing or Omoksee's. The horse's legs move all at different times.

Like the canter the horse will strike off with its non-leading hind foot. The inside hind foot hits the ground just before the outside front foot and ends with striking off of the leading leg; followed by a moment of complete suspension above the ground.

If you listen carefully you can hear the difference of an extended canter and a gallop. You can hear the fourth beat of the gallop versus the three beats of the canter.

Before you ever attempt to ride a gallop you need to be completely in control of your horse and fully capable of riding all the other gaits with ease. The gallop is very fast and can also be very dangerous.

Right lead gallop sequence:

First Beat-Hind left leg, Second beat-right hind leg, Third beat-left front leg, Fourth Beat-right front leg.

Diagram of the four beats of the gallop.

Beats of the horse gallop, a four beat movement:
The Right Lead Sequence:

Third Beat:
Left front leg   **Fourth Beat:**
Right front leg

First Beat:
Left hind leg   **Second Beat:**
Right hind leg

54

Left lead gallop sequence:

First Beat-Hind right leg, Second beat-left hind leg, Third beat-right front leg, Fourth beat-left front leg.

Diagram of the four beats of the gallop.

Beats of the horse gallop, a four beat movement:

The Left Lead Sequence:

Fourth Beat:
Left Front   **Third Beat:**
Right Front

Second Beat:
Left Hind   **First Beat:**
Right hind

56

Chapter Seven

Equine Blind Spots

Horses are considered a prey animal; and being a prey animal they have a fairly large range of vision to keep them protected from a predators attack. The horse's eye is the largest of any land mammal.

A horse's eyes are set on the side of their head to provide this wide range of vision. When working around horse's you need to be aware of their blind spots and how they may react if suddenly they become startled by something appearing in one of them. The way the horse sees is directly linked to how the horse reacts and thinks.

You should know the strengths and weaknesses of the horse's eyes and how they affect the way the horse reacts to things; especially when you begin training or working with any horse.

The blind spot directly in front of the horse is a large reason behind certain behaviors. Not wanting to load into a trailer, or suddenly striking without warning or pulling back on the halter.

When the horse goes to approach the trailer and is already leery of it then when the moment comes to trust and put his foot inside the horse can no longer see what he is putting his foot on.

When the horse suddenly strikes out seemingly without warning, it isn't because he didn't warn you, it just happened extremely fast and you may not have caught what startled the horse. It could have been, in some extremely spooky or over-reactive horse's case, a leaf blowing through the blind spot and coming out the other side that could set him off.

The horse's vision is largely affected by light and dark changes also. This is another reason for not loading well into a trailer. When a horse goes from outside to a dark setting or vice versa; it takes longer for the horse's eyes to adjust than it takes our eyes. This puts the horse on guard, and makes him more leery of things.

The blind spot along the sides of the horse are small, but can cause problems for someone starting a horse to ride. They need to be well accustomed to people moving and touching them in those areas before someone ever attempts to ride them.

Behind the horse is the largest of the blind spots and you need to be aware of it. Walking up behind the horse and startling it could be very dangerous, especially with a horse you don't know. You need to talk to the horse and let them know you are approaching them so you don't startle them. Even with your own horse that you may trust, you should practice safety and let that horse be aware of your presence as well. I find it is very important to teach children how to approach a horse. They are much shorter and that puts them in the kick range of the horse.

The following diagram will help give a better idea of where the blind spots are and what type of vision the horse has.

Diagram 1, blind spots of the horse.

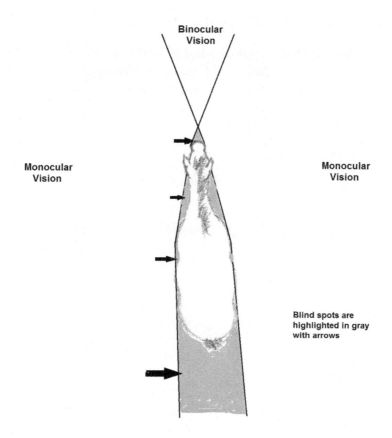

Blind spots are highlighted in gray with arrows

Binocular vision accounts for about 65 degrees of the horse's 350 degree vision. It is the vision directly in front of the horse; the horse uses this vision to spot a predator in the distance or to size up an object when moving to help the horse determine distance between it and an object.

Monocular vision accounts for the remaining 285 degrees of vision. The horse is a lateral eyed animal. Meaning their eyes are positioned on the side of their head. This vision helps to keep the horse aware of its surroundings.

Those are the basics of a horse's blind spots, they are very important to keep in mind at all times when you are around horses, whether you are on the ground or riding them.

Chapter 8

Safety Positions when Working Around Horses

Safety positions are invaluable, and the sooner one learns and ingrains them into your regular interaction with your horse, the safer you will be.

The very first and best thing you can do when working around a horse is to stay close to the horse. Staying close allows the horse to know you are there. It is also a lot safer if something does happen; you are less likely to sustain a bad injury.

Kind of like getting punched, if you are out at arm's length of a punch, it will hurt much more and do a lot more damage compared to being very close when it happens.

Another great safety measure is to keep at least one hand on the horse at all times when brushing or handling. This helps to keep the horse calm and also if the horse does suddenly move you will be able to notice any sudden changes in the horse, his muscles tightening or bracing; it will most likely help keep the horse off of you too.

Standing by the horse's shoulder is thought to be the safest position when handling a horse. It keeps you out of harm's way from the back feet and keeps you close to the horse's body; the front feet are usually striking out if something happens so most likely you will miss the connection with the strike as well. Staying by the shoulder isn't a guarantee that a horse can't hurt you, but it's the best bet you have.

When you approach any horse, be sure to always approach the horse from the side. This will help make sure the horse sees you. It is also a good idea to talk to the horse and let him know you are coming.

You don't want to approach a horse directly from the front or directly from the back. This puts you in harm's way from both directions. Your best place to approach is from the side at about a 45 degree angle to the horse's shoulder.

Diagram 1, a safe way to approach a horse.

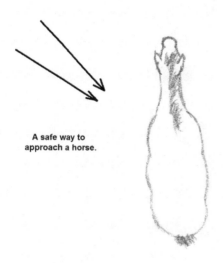

You also never want to approach or stand directly behind a horse. This is your horse's blind spot and the deadly kick zone. Many people have been seriously injured or killed by being kicked by a horse.

Diagram 2 unsafe places to approach.

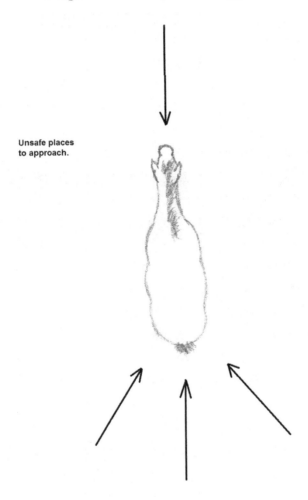

Unsafe places to approach.

When you need to move to the other side of your horse from the back side; place your hand on the horse's hindquarter on the side you are currently on. Keep your hand in the same spot for the whole movement, while remaining as close to the horse as possible. It is good to talk to the horse while you are moving around it, that way he knows where you are and that you are moving, lessening the chance you will startle the horse.

Or if you don't want to be in harm's way at all, walk well beyond the horses kicking range and give plenty of space. Their legs can reach a lot farther out than you would expect if the horse is provoked to kick out.

Never duck under the horse's belly or neck. Especially when a horse is tied; this is a recipe for disaster. When you duck under the horse you pass through the blind spot and suddenly appear on the other side. This puts you in danger of being stomped or crushed. If you startle a horse while it is tied, the horse may pull back and from there the only action after pulling back is to jump directly forward or fall down; neither or which will be good for you.

When you are beginning with horses it is a good idea to always have someone around while you are working with the horse. Things can go wrong very quickly with horses. Even experienced riders should have someone know where they are and what they are doing at all times.

Diagram 3 safe places to stand when grooming.

Safe places to stand when grooming.

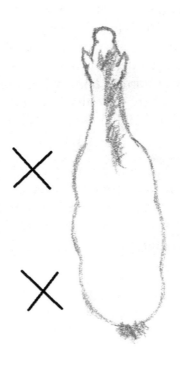

When grooming the back of your horse, stand close to the hip and keep one hand on the horse at all times.

~~~

Safe ways to lead a horse are first; stay beside the horse, behind the poll but in front of his left shoulder. Your right hand should have a hold of the lead shank directly under the horses jaw. Your left hand should hold the excess rope, be sure your left hand doesn't become tangled in the rope. If you hand ever does become tangled in a rope, you must relax your hand completely. Do not tense your hand up at all. This will usually help to release your hand from a rope. Always know what your horse's body is doing in relation to what your own is doing.

Second, have the horse follow directly behind you; several feet back. This method needs a horse that is respectful enough to not crowd your personal space. It can be a very safe position if you do it correctly. Walking in front of the horse with some distance between you, the horse has multiple ways of moving if he is startled. Be careful how much distance you have between you and the horse; if the horse spooks past you and has enough rope to completely pass you, you will be in line for getting kicked by the horse.

Wear appropriate clothing when working around horses. This should be clothing that covers you and protects you well.

Boots are a must-have item; they will help protect your feet and ankles. If you are riding, the boots should have some kind of a heel to keep your foot from going through the stirrup. If you are on the ground, be careful and aware of where your feet are at all times. Also it isn't a good idea to wear steel-toed shoes, because if stepped on they could cut your toes off completely.

Other things that are crucial to learn is how to safely load and unload your horse from a trailer. It is also equally crucial for your horse to know how to safely load and unload. Even if you don't travel or have a trailer you horse should be able to trailer safely. If you need to use a trailer to get your horse to a vet's, it is better to be prepared than sorry you haven't worked with your horse before needing it to load. Sometimes it can take a great deal of work to get a horse loaded the first time.

You also should be able to tie your horse properly. Improperly tying a horse can result in injury to you or the horse. Never tie your horse too high, or too low. A safe height to tie your horse is usually eye level if the horse is standing normally. This is usually 5 feet or above; you may need to adjust for shorter horses.

Also never tie your horse to an object that can be moved. Such as a rail on a fence rather than a post, door handles, lawn chairs, something with sharp edges that could cut the horse, etc.

Chapter Nine

Parts of the Saddle, English and Western

Saddles have been around for a very long time and while horses are the most common use for a saddle in the United States, animals such as camels and elephants have had saddles specifically made for them as well.

Saddles began very simply, but today there are many styles and types available and all must be sized to both the horse and rider. The basic types available to modern man are the English and western saddles.

Saddles have been used as symbols of status and pride since man first developed them. They have evolved a long way since the first introduction of a girth and a fleece pad.

A saddle regardless of type needs to fit the horse and rider well. Saddle fitting is an art and is best performed by a saddle maker or saddle specialist. Custom saddles made to the individual and the horse, are of course usually the best fit you can get. These are also usually very expensive.

You can get by just fine with a manufactured saddle if you select it carefully by the type of horse you have, what you intend the saddle for. You'll probably still need to make a few adjustments to assure a good fit.

The width of the saddle is the primary way of measuring fit to a horse; although length of the tree and proper balance should also be taken into account. The gullet of the saddle must clear the horse's withers, but must be wide enough to not pinch the horse's back. Too wide can also be a problem when fitting your horse.

The tree of the saddle must be positioned so that the tree bars (in English or western saddles) do not interfere with the movement of the horses shoulders. The seat should be positioned so that when the rider is riding correctly it places the rider over the horse's center of balance.

The bars of the saddle must be the correct length. They shouldn't place pressure past the horse's last rib; nor should they be too short either. A short tree with an unbalanced rider can lead to irregular pressure points on the horse.

A saddle must be tried on a horse to assure proper fit. Using different types of saddle pads can help to correct minor saddle fitting issues. Still you need to make your choice wisely, there is absolutely no pad or special fitting that will help a poor-fitting saddle.

One saddle will not fit all animals. That's just the way it is; a saddle may also not fit an individual horse after a period of time has passed. The horse's condition could change due to age or fitness, thus changing the muscular structure of the back. After awhile you may need to make adjustments to be sure of a good fit.

There are many ways of fitting a saddle to the rider. The most popular way is the seat's measurement although the length and placement of the flaps or fenders of the saddle (affecting a person's leg position and the way the individual person sits in the saddle), needs to be taken into account as well.

Having either too long or too short of a seat can cause discomfort to the rider and can interfere with the safety of the rider on the horse. The width of the saddle is also a factor when finding the correct fit of a saddle. Any well-fitted saddle should be wide enough to support the rider's seat bones, but not so wide that it causes discomfort. Note that most saddles are not sold in relation to width but only in length of the seat. The only reliable way to find if the saddle fits you is to sit in it.

Balance is also an important factor; a properly engineered saddle places the rider over the horse's center of balance for that specific discipline (roping, trail use, etc.). A poor-fitting saddle often leaves the rider feeling like they are sliding backwards or are constantly trying to move themselves uphill. Less common (but still a concern) is the saddle that leaves the rider feeling they are being pushed forward onto the horse's neck.

Caring for your saddle is also a large part of making sure you get the most out of your saddle's life.

Storing the saddle properly will help to keep the leather in good condition. You also should be careful of the temperature at which you store your saddle. It should be relatively cool and away from direct sunlight, while maintaining a constant temperature. If your saddle is inside be careful it isn't next to a heat source. That can dry out the leather and cause cracking; cracks in the leather need to be repaired because the leather is getting weak and could be dangerous when the saddle is being used.

While keeping your tack with your horse sometimes doesn't allow for the most perfect conditions, you can still keep your saddle in good shape by cleaning and oiling the saddle on a regular basis. Regularly cleaning the saddle helps to keep dirt and scum from building up and prevents future problems.

The English Saddle

Now we will take a look at the parts of an English saddle. There are many styles, shapes, and sizes of English saddle but, all contain the same basic makeup.

The following is a diagram of the English saddle and its parts.

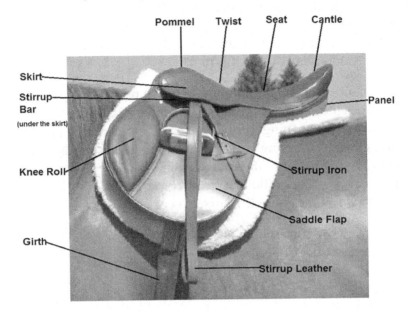

Just like in our previous chapters here is a list of the saddle's parts. Use these as a reference for the next page.

English Saddle Parts

1. Skirt
2. Stirrup Bar (under the skirt)
3. Knee roll
4. Girth
5. Stirrup leather
6. Saddle flap
7. Stirrup Iron
8. Panel
9. Cantle
10. Seat
11. Twist
12. Pommel

Diagram of the parts of the English saddle; label the words on the correct line from the list.

The Western Saddle

Just like the English saddle there are many styles and fits of the western saddle but they all have the same basic makeup.

The western saddle was originated from the Spanish. The Spanish cowboys developed the western saddle for their every day work that they needed to do. The western saddle was built to be sturdy and fashioned with a stout horn for tying off to things, (such a holding a steer for the cowboys or dragging something).

Study the diagrams of the western saddle to learn all the parts of the saddle and their names.

This is a diagram of the western saddle and its parts.

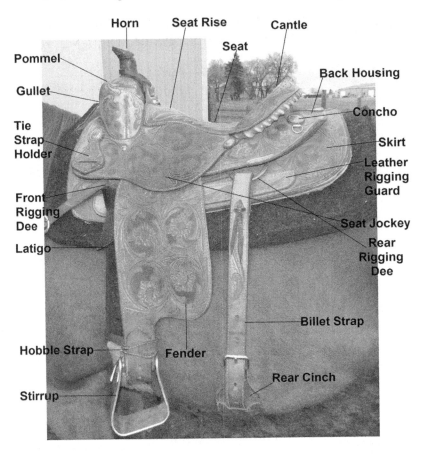

Western saddle parts:

1. Horn
2. Seat Rise
3. Seat
4. Cantle
5. Back Housing
6. Concho
7. Skirt

8. Leather Rigging Guard
9. Seat Jockey
10. Rear Rigging Dee
11. Billet Strap
12. Rear Cinch
13. Fender
14. Stirrup
15. Hobble strap
16. Latigo
17. Front Rigging Dee
18. Tie Strap Holder
19. Gullet
20. Pommel

Just like with the English saddle, label the parts from the list on the other page and put them where they are supposed to be.

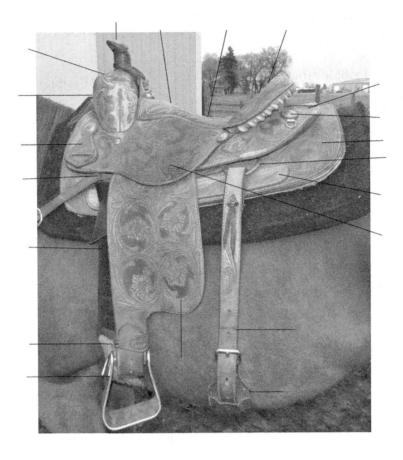

The western saddle has a few more parts than the English saddle does but, all are important to know.

I hope this chapter helps you to learn the basics of both English and western saddles.

Chapter Ten

Halters & Bridles

Halters are a form of head gear used to restrain or tie up animals. The halter fits behind the ears and the poll, then over the muzzle of the animal.

Halters have been around since the first form of domestication of animals. They aren't as well researched as the bridle or hackamore, thus less is known about their exact origin.

Halters can be classified into two broad categories, depending on (a) the type of material, (b) whether it is flat or round.

Many traditional materials used to create a halter include leather, rawhide, cotton, or various kinds of rope. They are sometimes made from synthetic materials like nylon or polyester. Most rope type halters are made of one long rope tied together in specific locations to create the halter.

Halters have also been fashioned out of things like baling twine and chains.

Don't confuse the halter with the bridle. A halter is meant to be used when the horse isn't being ridden. It aids in tying, leading and many other things one may do on the ground with their horse, while a bridle is for riding or driving the animal.

A halter is much safer for the horse on the ground. Especially when tying the horse up. The bit can cause severe damage to a horse's mouth if tied with the bridle. Also a bridle will break easier than a halter, making it much more dangerous to tie up a horse with it.

A common halter is the flat web halter. This halter is usually sewn together where the webbing meets the hardware. The halter consists of a nose band connected to the cheek strap, which connects to the throat latch and the crown piece. Usually there's a connector strap in between the nose band and the throat latch.

This is a diagram of a web halter.

The rope halter is simply a long rope tied together to create a halter. This halter has the same basic sections and all the parts are the same as the web halter. Most rope halters have no metal parts with the occasional exception of a ring to hook the lead rope into.

One thing you need to be certain of is how you fasten the

halter on the horse.

The rope halter is fastened with a sheet bend also known as a weavers knot. It's strong, fast and easy knot to tie.

The following diagram is a rope halter and how to tie the knot properly on the horse.

Step 1 Pull the Crown piece through the loop.

Step 2 Take the tail of the crown piece, and loop it *under* the first loop.

Step 3 place the tail back through the loop you just created.

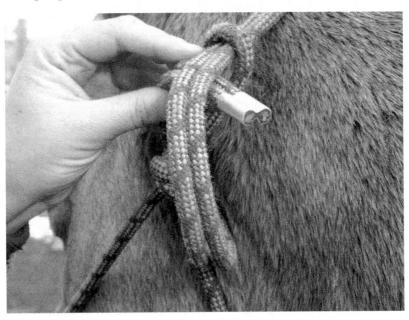

Step 4 Final step tighten and tuck away the ends.

Bridles

A bridle is a piece of equipment used to direct a horse while riding or driving. The bridle includes both the headstall that holds it up and the reins which are attached to the bit.

A bridle with a nose band instead of a bit is called a hackamore or in some cases a bitless bridle. There are many different designs for this type of bridle, though all have a nose piece which puts pressure on the nose to allow for controlling the horse.

The English Bridle

The English bridle is most commonly used in English riding. It is usually referred to as a snaffle bridle, it is a basic type of bridle with one bit and one set of reins attached. Although it is referred to as a snaffle bridle any form of bit can be used on the bridle. The English bridle almost always has a noseband or cavesson.

The Pelham bridle is another English bridle that is also a single bit but, it has two separate sets of reins directing the horse. There is also the double bridle in English riding. This is usually only seen in dressage or other forms of formal completion. It will have two bits and two sets of reins.

This is a diagram of the parts of the English bridle.

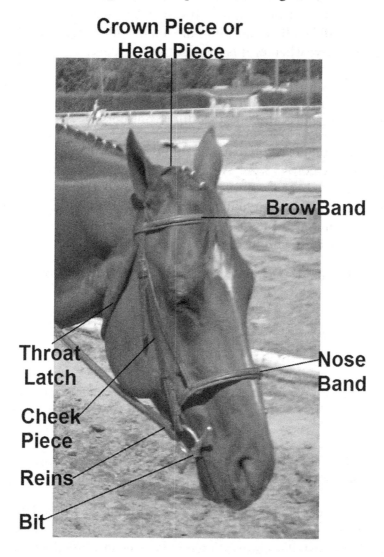

83

The length of each individual piece of the bridle needs to be adjusted to fit the horse's head. Fitting a bridle has to be done specifically to the individual horse. An ill fitting headstall can make the horse uncomfortable. It can also be dangerous. You could have difficulty controlling the horse with a bridle that isn't fitted properly; whether it is too tight or too loose.

There are limitations to adjustments of certain parts of the headstall, which is why there are so many sizes and types offered when finding the correct headstall for your horse.

The bit and brow band are at set lengths and should be selected for the correct size. A bit that is too narrow is very uncomfortable to the horse. A bit that is too wide makes the bit slide around in the horse's mouth and can provide you with less control. You can help this sometimes by adding bit guards to the bridle. This will make the bit narrower.

If the brow band is too short it can cause the brow band to rub the ears and cause the horse irritation.

The Western Bridle

The western bridle is used in western style riding. The western bridle almost never has a nose band unless it is an added piece of equipment for that specific horse. In that case the nose band is usually a tie down that is completely separate from the bridle.

Sometimes the western bridle doesn't have a brow band either. Instead it has what is known as a one or double ear headstall.

Almost all working western bridles have a throat latch but some headstalls used in showing do not. The throat latch helps keep the headstall securely on the horse's head when the horse is moving. A good measurement when adjusting the throat latch is that 3 or 4 fingers can be inside the throat latch. This allows the horse to move and breathe properly.

This is a diagram of the parts of the Western Bridle.

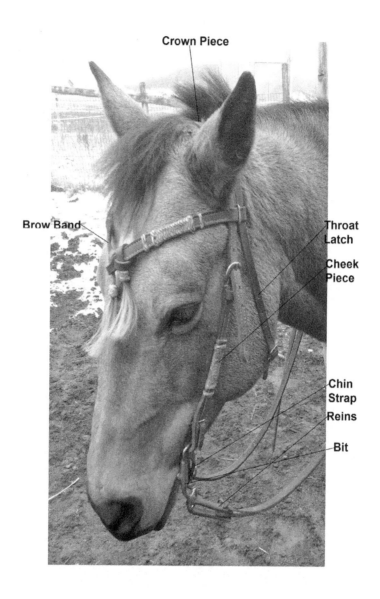

Chapter 11

Basic Feeding of Horses

When feeding horses there are a lot of factors that come into play. You'll need to consider not only in the nutrients they need to receive but also the weather conditions, time of year, and the size and age of the horse.

On very important subject I would like to touch on in this chapter and one you should remember carefully is to have regular dental work done on your horse. They are finding a lot of things in relation to a horse's teeth and how it acts, not just on the horse's nutritional health and ability to digest food properly. But also how the horse reacts to things such as training and the attitude the horse has about it. Imagine how having an infected or rotting tooth and how it would affect your attitude!

Your horse's poor teeth can cause problems like head tossing, or rearing, and/or bucking. It is also important to have someone with a good reputation work on your horse's teeth. Not all dental experts are the same and some are better than others just like farriers and veterinarians. When looking for a dental expert in your area, you should ask around at several barns. You will more than likely get some good recommendations that way.

When a horse is young, they are constantly shedding their teeth and growing in new ones. Sometimes during this process the caps of the old teeth become stuck or lodged on the new teeth. This creates pain for the horse and difficulty chewing. It can also result in the horse not being able to digest its food properly resulting in malnourishment.

There are also teeth called wolf teeth that can grow in and cause the horse problems from a bit hitting the teeth. These should be removed by a dental expert. Wolf teeth are typically used by the horse in the wild for fighting with other horses, so most of the time they are present in males, but sometimes they can also grow in females. They are relatively useless in the domestic horse.

It is very important to keep your horse's teeth working properly and to know if there are any concerns. Teeth can have serious health impacts. If the horse is eating too quickly and not chewing its food properly because of a painful tooth or has a sore mouth caused by a sharp tooth your horse may choke or colic from the improperly chewed food.

Having such a large throat can be a serious problem when a horse chokes. Getting the feed that is lodged in the horse's throat out can cause irritation to the throat itself, resulting in scar tissue which makes the horse more susceptible to choking again in the future.

Dental problems can also create a serious infection that can spread throughout the horse's body.

Getting your horse's teeth checked regularly is very important. "Regular" varies from individual to individual. Some horse's can go 2-3 years between visits, but I've heard of other horses that need their teeth checked twice or more a year. It just depends on the individual.

When I first purchase a horse, one of the first things I look into is when it had its teeth done last or if ever. From there, depending on the last time, it gets taken care of very soon. That way I know what the horse has going on with its teeth.

Feed Choices

There are so many types of feed out there today, most of which are good. But, which one should you feed to your horse? What does your horse need? Feeding and nutrition is an extremely important part of a horse owner's responsibility. Don't get too stressed out about it though. There are many easy ways to learn what is best for your horse.

When feeding horse's it is important to remember that there are six basic nutrition requirements; carbohydrates, protein, fat, vitamins, minerals and of course water.

Water is the single most important nutrient for most animals. They have to have water to survive; if they don't have enough of any of the other nutrients they are just deficient in that area. Although long term deficiency of any nutrient isn't good for anyone; water is definitely the most crucial.

An adult horse will usually drink anywhere from 5-15 gallons of water a day, sometimes even more. Water needs to be accessible at all times. Horses that don't drink enough water are more prone to having intestinal problems, such as impactions and other forms of colic.

The rest of your horse's diet should be formulated based on what it needs from the other nutrients. Each individual horse has different requirements, based off the horse's size, body mass, age and work load.

Carbohydrates are going to be the main staple in your horse's diet. You can divide carbohydrates into structural and non-structural carbs. Structural carbohydrates are your fiber; while non-structural carbohydrates are your sugars and starches. The horse's intestines are specifically designed to be able to break that roughage down. That is why the horse receives so much of its nutrition from hay and grasses.

It is very important to feed good quality hay that is free from mold and dust and which was cut at an appropriate age and length to get the maximum benefit for your horse.

Hay that is too small or too large a grain can cause health problems in the horse like an impaction. Hay that is cut too late in its growth stage has little to no nutrition left in it.

Sugars and starches are primarily found in grains; this concentrated version provides more energy than your typical non-structural sugars and starches found in your hay or grass. Thus the name concentrated on most of the packaging. Grains serve their purpose by supplying an area that is deficient in something and can provide more energy for the horse. Feeding grain excessively can also have adverse affects, such as colic or ulcers.

You need to always remember horses were meant to eat and process a roughage-based diet. Therefore, grains should only be fed to supplement your forage, and to help meet nutritional requirements that just eating forage cannot.

The horse should always be fed at least 1.5 to 2% of its body weight in roughage, on a daily basis. An absolute minimum of 1% its body weight; it takes at least this much to keep a horse's digestive system moving correctly.

Protein is necessary for body growth and maintenance. Proteins are composed of amino acids; the proteins that the body makes have very specific amino acid sequences.

Some believe that protein can give a horse too much energy or excessive energy. While the real truth of the matter is that horses have a very difficult time breaking down protein and utilizing it in their body. Protein requirements depend on age and work load. A working horse with a heavy work load will usually need a protein percentage of about 12%, while horses that are in more of a maintenance cycle need between 8-12%. A young growing horse will need anywhere from 12-18%; same with lactating mares.

If you feed horses a higher level of protein than they need the horse will not use up the protein and it will be broken down and excreted in their urine. This becomes ammonia, which is not good for stabled horses especially.

Forage is also a good source for protein, so feeding a good quality hay whether it be a grass hay (10-16% protein) or a good quality alfalfa hay(16-22% protein).

Fat is an easily digestible source of energy for a horse. It is important when adding fat to a horse's diet that you make sure to meet all of his other nutrient needs as well and not just the horse's energy needs.

Vitamins are critically important organic compounds. They must be present in the body to allow important reactions to take place so that the animal may live.

Vitamins can be divided into two groups, water-soluble and fat-soluble. Water soluble vitamins contain the B vitamins, while the fat-soluble vitamins contain A, D, E, and K.

The horse typically synthesizes all the vitamins that it needs and it usually isn't that necessary to supplement a horse with vitamins. However, vitamin deficiencies can lead to health problems so it is important to pay attention and know about vitamins and what they do. It is also important you check your feed labeling, to make sure if you do need to supplement your horse that the feed has the proper requirements and that all the vitamins needed are there.

It is also good to recognize that an extreme excess of vitamins is not good either. It needs to be the correct amount. Water-soluble vitamins in excess are usually just excreted out the urine but, fat-soluble vitamins are stored in the horse's fat tissue, so that they are readily available when the horse needs them. Excess of this type can create toxicity. Exercise good judgment when you are feeding higher concentrates of vitamins.

In most cases a good forage program will provide all that your horse needs.

Minerals are material that must be present in the body for the body to function properly.

Know that your horse's mineral needs will change many times throughout its life, depending upon the horse's age and current status.

Again, forage will also provide minerals. However, in some cases additional minerals added into a horse's diet can provide some desirable benefits. Zinc, copper, and biotin for example have been credited in strengthening hooves when fed excessively.

Even with the benefits though, you should be careful because excessive feeding of minerals can also lead to toxicity and can cause other health concerns, along with making it harder for the horse to absorb other minerals.

Having salt on hand for your horse is also very important in maintaining the horse's diet. A mineral salt combination is sometimes a good way to provide the horse with some extra minerals without going overboard. A horse needs salt in their diet to help maintain them, especially if the horse is sweating a lot.

You also should be careful of your phosphorus to calcium ratio if you are feeding grain. Phosphorus is usually low in grasses and hay and you rarely would ever have a problem. But, in grains or vitamin/mineral supplements phosphorus is usually high.

When phosphorus is high in relation to calcium, calcium will be pulled from the bone into the bloodstream to balance everything out. If you are feeding a single grain such as oats, you can have the opposite problem. So be sure your horse has enough calcium in his diet as well.

Another mineral consideration you should take into account is how much does your horse sweat? Is it none or is it a lot?

Horses that have a moderate to intense work load lose electrolytes and can need supplementation to replace the lost electrolytes (like potassium). They also need access to salt on a regular basis to help replace what has been sweated out.

Feeding your horse is very much up to you. There are many ways you can feed a horse and many great ways of feeding a horse. Be careful of grains that are rich and have too much of certain fats, vitamins or minerals.

But most importantly, provide good quality forage for your horse and most of your health concerns are taken care of. It depends on the case of course, but just like with our own diet, if you keep things basic the better off you seem to be.

The basics will keep you from over feeding a supplement and causing poisoning to the horse. Of course just like us we often times require a little more than the basics, but keep it as close to them as you can and things will be a little simpler.

Chapter 12

Common Diseases, Vaccinations & Parasites

Before we get started with this chapter, I want to make note that I am not a veterinarian, nor do I claim to be. These are just facts about certain illnesses a horse can have or come into contact with. I have been around these illnesses before and being in the horse industry for quite awhile I'm very familiar with them. If you feel you need veterinary assistance please contact them as soon as possible and make arrangements for your horse. Thank you.

In essence I want to touch base a little on what common diseases are out there, a little bit about them, what they do and their signs. Then I want to cover vaccinating your horse to protect against these deadly diseases and also a little about some common parasites, what they affect and common treatments of them.

Tetanus

About 50-75% of horses that end up with tetanus don't live after contracting it.

It usually gets started from a deep cut or puncture wound; anything from a nail in the bottom of the hoof, to a cut caused by running into or kicking something.

It usually takes tetanus about one to three weeks to set in. Most of the time it is a wound that has foreign material in it. Any deep wound that is not sterile is a possible entry site for the threat of tetanus, deep wounds that aren't cleaned or, a deep surgical site is a perfect place for the spores to grow. Tetanus is a very scary scenario to be involved with let alone to just think about.

Tetanus also referred to as "lock jaw" attacks the horse's nervous system. The horse's who signs of the disorder progress quickly are usually the ones that don't recover from the disease and don't make it.

The toxins travel along the nerves until they reach the central nervous system. Then muscle spasms begin, the spasms are continuous. The more advanced signs of the spasms include muscles of the head and face contract, ears are erect and pointed backwards, nostrils flared, and the muscles of the lips are pulled back like the horse is smiling. The neck may become rigid and the back muscles contract; the tail will begin to stick straight out. The horse may drool because it is having trouble being able to swallow. It was called lockjaw because the jaws of the horse appear locked with the spasms and the horse can no longer eat.

The best way to stay safe from tetanus is to keep your horse up to date on its vaccines. Although, there isn't a 100% chance on anything, it is proven to work very well and has greatly reduced the likelihood of contracting tetanus. As with most things, it's better to be safe than sorry, and far easier in the long run to have your vaccination program current and up to date.

Another precaution against Tetanus is to keep your horse facilities free of as many sharp or dangerous objects as possible. As any good horse owner knows though, a horse can find ways to hurt itself in a padded room.

Equine Encephalomyelitis

Eastern & Western

Eastern Encephalomyelitis or sleeping sickness is present in North, South, Central United States and the Caribbean.

The virus is capable of infecting a large range of animals including mammals, birds, reptiles, and amphibians. The virus is maintained by a bird/mosquito cycle. The mosquitoes feed on the blood of birds and as things warm up in the summer, more mosquitoes and more birds become infected.

Transmission of the virus is from mosquitoes to other mammals. The mosquitoes act as a host to bring the virus from one animal to another. People can also become infected from the bite of an infected mosquito. In people the fatality rate is 35-65% and there is no cure.

Although a horse, human, or other mammals can contract the virus from one simple bite of an infected mosquito, they don't carry enough of the virus in their blood stream to infect other mosquitoes that may bite them.

Symptoms in the horse occur one to three weeks after first contracting the virus. It begins with a fever that usually last 24-48 hours. Nervous signs appear during the fever period, restlessness, sensitivity to sound, excitement. Brain lesions appear, causing drowsiness, droopy ears, circling, walking aimlessly, and inability to swallow. Paralysis usually sets in causing the horse to have difficulty raising its head. After that complete paralysis sets in and usually the horse dies shortly after that; typically two to four days after symptoms appear sometimes seizures and coma accompany paralysis as well. Mortality among horses with the eastern strain is around 70-90%.

Western Encephalomyelitis is much like the eastern strain of the virus. They are both transmitted by mosquitoes and interspecies. Both viruses affect the nervous system of the horse. Human mortality is actually quite low compared to eastern; western is at 4% in people. In horses Mortality is also much lower, 20-40%.

Again the best way to protect your horse is to have a current vaccination regimen. It is not always fool proof but, it's better than having no protection at all.

Influenza

Equine influenza occurs all over the world. It can spread very quickly, and has an almost 100% success rate at infecting a population of horses not vaccinated against it. Thus, it has a high rate at which it can be transmitted from one horse to another. It takes about one to five days to fully develop.

Horses typically develop a runny nose, fever, have a dry cough, act depressed and are reluctant to eat or drink for many days. Typically the horse will usually recover in two to three weeks.

The best remedy for avoiding the equine flu is vaccination and keeping the horse in sanitary conditions while being aware of any out breaks in your area. It's especially crucial to vaccinate if you plan to travel (for your horse's safety and others).

Rhinopneumonitis

(AKA rhino, equine herpes virus)

Like other herpes viruses, it will be with an infected animal for life. These horses are usually the source for infection of new foals, or young horses; the disease can lay dormant in the animal a long time and you won't even know it is there.

The spread of equine herpes virus is a lot like that of humans. The affected horse may harbor the disease without any obvious symptoms. Direct contact is usually the most common method for contracting the disease.

Symptoms include, fever, loss of appetite, discharge from the nose. Without antibiotic treatment the horse is exposed to the risk of secondary infections as well.

In pregnant mares certain strains of the virus cause abortions; it can also make it virtually impossible for the mare to conceive.

Although once a horse gets equine herpes virus there is no cure, it is still highly recommended to vaccinate to help keep the disease from spreading any further and to protect horses that are at a higher risk of contracting the disease.

West Nile Virus

West Nile is an inflammation of the central nervous system. West Nile virus was only found in Africa, Eastern Europe, and Western Asia prior to 1999. It was then identified to be in the United States.

People and animals can become infected with the virus by being bitten by an affected mosquito. Mosquitoes pick the virus up when they take blood from infected birds; and transfer the virus to a person or animal when they take blood from them.

Horses appear to be a species that is susceptible in getting the virus. When a horse does become ill with the virus, it affects the central nervous system of the animal and can cause symptoms of encephalitis. Clinical signs include and can be any or all of the above, loss of appetite, depression, fever, weakness, paralysis, aimless wandering, and seizures, walking in circles, excessive excitability, or coma.

The best way to prevent West Nile Virus is to eliminate mosquito breeding grounds. The fewer the mosquitoes the better; making sure all buckets, pots, pans, extra water tanks are emptied of stagnant water which is the perfect breeding ground for mosquitoes. Your other best bet of avoiding it is to keep your horse vaccinated for protection from the virus. Not 100% guaranteed like all other vaccines.

Strangles

(Also Equine Distemper & Shipping Fever)

Strangles is a highly contagious upper respiratory tract infection in horses. The disease is spread from nasal discharge when the horse gets it on feeders, in waters, fences, or just touches another horse.

All horses can contract the disease and fairly easily. But, like the flu in humans, the disease is much more susceptible in younger or older horses.

Signs of Strangles include fever, nasal discharge, swelling around the throat and throat latch. It can result in loss of appetite and the horse may become depressed.

Treatments include penicillin and other forms of antibiotics as well. Once the abscesses burst it is very important to keep the area clean and free of contamination. An iodine solution is usually the best way to clean the area around and in the wound.

The average length of time for the disease to run its course is about three to four weeks.

Immediate isolation of an infected horse is key in keeping the disease from spreading. Disinfecting anything the horse has or may have come into contact with is crucial.

Again the best way to protect your horse against Strangles before it ever begins is with vaccinations. They have both an intramuscular vaccination and an intranasal form.

These are just a few the basic diseases you should vaccinate your horse against. There are many more you may need to consider for your area. The best way to figure out which ones are best for you is to contact your veterinarian and find out what they recommend for your area. There are also many people that don't believe in vaccinating their horses. In the end it is your call.

I travel with my horses a lot and take all the precautions I can to protect them. At this time the best prevention is to vaccinate.

Regular Worming schedules for your horse and Parasites to look for

Every horse's needs are different for worming. Even in a group of horses that are in the same pasture or barn, each individual is different in how they respond to worms and how they are affected.

There are many types of wormers on the market today. All have different dosages for each type of parasite and different times of the year that they are more affective.

The best way to determine your horse's worming needs is to have a veterinarian perform a fecal matter test. In this test your veterinarian will get a worm egg count and types of eggs to help put a deworming program together for your horse.

Worms can get a resistance over time to dewormers which reduce the wormer's effectiveness. The best way to avoid this is to worm enough to help maintain a healthy horse, yet not so much to give the worms time to build up a resistance.

Internal parasites are usually transferred from manure so keeping pastures, corrals, and stalls clean is one of the best methods of reducing your worm infestation. Harrowing pastures also helps to keep them under control.

Reducing the number of horses that are in a pen or on the pasture helps as well as rotating horses between pastures. Also, using feeders to feed your horse aids in reducing worm infestation.

Worms and Parasites

Pinworms are usually found in the horse's environment. Such things as fence posts and different grooming objects can carry them. Pinworms deposit their eggs around the anus of the horse and this causes intense itching around the affected area. From this the horse may rub out its tail completely or cause other damage to the rump or tail.

Ascarids or large round worms are found in the small intestine. The adults lay the eggs which are then passed out through the manure. The eggs become infectious in about two weeks, then the horse grazes around the contagious area and they travel in through the horse's liver and lungs, where they are coughed up and swallowed back into the small intestine.

Bots are the young maggot larva of the botfly. The botfly looks like a blonde, fuzzy bumble bee. They lay their eggs on the front legs and long hairs of the face. The horse then ends up ingesting the eggs. They attach themselves to the tongue and insides of the mouth and from there migrate to the lining of the stomach, where they stay for a long time.

Large Strongyles or blood worms are usually very strongly attached to the walls of the large intestine. Like the round worms they lay many eggs which pass out of the horse through its manure. From there the larva climb up grass and are ingested by the horse. The larva affect the large arteries of the intestines in the horse, causing blood clots to form then release resulting in pain and colic in the horse.

Tapeworms, are ingested when the horse is grazing and eats the parasite. Tapeworms can cause serious malnourishment, digestive problems and can lead to colic. Tapeworms are difficult to locate in a horse.

These are some of the worms you should see on the dewormers packaging when purchasing your dewormer.

The old way of worming was to worm your horse every 6-8 weeks but they are finding this helps the worms build up a tolerance to the dewormers on the market.

I de-worm my horses every quarter. If I have younger or older horses I may increase that to 6 or more times a year (depending on the individual horse and their needs). A new horse gets de-wormed, long before it's introduced to the rest of the herd.

Your horse may be fine on a quarterly schedule or it may need to be de-wormed every 6 weeks. The best ways to determine this is to pay attention to your horse and to consult with a veterinarian.

Another type of wormer is a daily feed thru type. Feed thru wormers can be very expensive to maintain. Ultimately, the choice is yours.

One thing I would add is to read the label of the dewormer very carefully. Make sure that it is safe for your horse, pony, or young horse to have. There are certain kinds of dewormers that are extremely dangerous to young horses and ponies. So before you give your horse the dewormer be sure it is safe.

Chapter 13

Closing Thoughts

We have covered some basics of having a horse and knowing different things about them. We began with learning the parts of the horse and parts of the hoof.

We also covered a few common hoof problems and diseases. Some of which are quite scary to deal with. But, if you know a little about them most of the time you can easily treat them or avoid them completely.

We've examined the blemishes and unsoundness's a horse can have, the beats of the horse, blind spots that can affect a horse and the way it thinks, and safety positions when working around horses. We also learned the parts of saddles and bridles and some basic feeding, common diseases, and parasite preventions.

With these basics, I would like to add, as a horseman you must always be learning and open to new ideas. There is no perfect, "set-in-stone" method for having a healthy, happy horse. You will find your own way of doing things and have your very own regimen but when you look back you will find you took a little from this person and something else from that person. Even if you only pick up one thing from someone it's still one thing you didn't know before.

Most important of all is keep things simple and fun. You

need to learn all the technical stuff but don't let it overwhelm you or deter you from having a fantastic relationship with your horse.

I hope you enjoyed this book and can keep it as a reference. I thank you for reading my book. I look forward to creating my next one.

I thoroughly enjoyed writing this and putting everything together. Thanks again and many happy trails to you!

Made in the USA
Middletown, DE
08 August 2019